How to Buy Real Estate for 40% OFF

Break Into The Secret World of Note Investing

By Scott Carson

General Notice

Publisher: Lulu

While they have made every effort to verify the information here, the author assumes no responsibility for errors in, omissions from or different interpretation of the subject matter. This information may be subject to varying laws and practices in different areas, states and countries. The reader assumes all responsibility for use of the information.

The author shall in no event be held liable to any party for any damages arising directly or indirectly from any use of this material. Every effort has been made to accurately represent this product and its potential and there is no guarantee that you will earn any money using these techniques.

ISBN: 978-1-365-99101-1

CONTENTS

THE HUGE POTENTIAL OF NOTE INVESTING

"Ninety percent of all millionaires become so through owning real estate. More money has been made in real estate than in all industrial investments combined. The wise young man or wage earner of today invests his money in real estate."

Andrew Carnegie

In this book, I share with you how you can take advantage of the opportunity to earn big returns on property without all the hassles and problems that the traditional approach to property investment can often bring.

Essentially I'll show you how to *buy property at substantial discounts and in a way that allows you to profit significantly from the forthcoming new economic storms* rather than be a victim of them.

You're probably already aware that property has been proven to be one of the best ways to invest over many years.

But maybe you've tried investing in property and become aware of the challenges it can often involve, such as:

×   Difficulties of finding suitable properties

×   Time and cost of redeveloping them

×   Short-term, unpredictable fluctuations in value

×   Problems in finding suitable tenants for rental

×   Challenges of getting suitable finance

What if, instead, I could show you:

✓   How to buy high-quality properties at substantial discounts to what unsophisticated investors are paying

✓   How you could turn these investments round quickly to produce an attractive return on your investment

✓   How you could do this without all the costs and hassles of fix and flip... with the prospect of significantly higher return

✓   Why there is a huge Mortgage Meltdown coming soon that makes this a massive opportunity... yet it is one known to only a relative handful of small investors

✓   How to avoid being a victim in this coming economic tsunami and instead profit from the past mistakes of the big banks and financial companies

Discover the World of Note Investing

Welcome to the world of note investing, which is a bit of an unknown niche hidden inside of the massive real estate and investing universe.

In this book, I'm going to outline:

- What note investing is
- How it works
- Why it can be an attractive investment
- The big opportunity that's opening up in this market
- How you can profit from this massive forthcoming change

But first, let me start with a quick overview of notes and note investing.

- A "note" is the legal paper behind a mortgage or loan from a bank or other financial institution

- The original issuing banks often sell these notes to other institutions or investors

- If the borrower falls behind in their payments, the note is said to be "nonperforming" and, at some stage, the bank owning that note may want to get it off their books (they are often legally required to do this)

➤ The bank then sells that note to other investors at a substantial discount, at a price often significantly less than the value of the actual property behind it

➤ The investor then seeks to profit from the deal either by selling that property at a profit or by negotiating a rental deal either with the existing occupant or a new tenant

The Coming Meltdown

When approached correctly, this approach to property investment can offer greater profits with less hassle than traditional approaches.

And here's the thing...

Property values... and the ability of people to pay their mortgages... have been protected by the bailouts provided by the government that have allowed banks to keep mortgage interest rates relatively low in recent years.

The effect of these bailouts is now winding down and many more banks will be left with non-performing notes to add to those they already have in place from the last Mortgage Meltdown.

This is going to present huge problems for many.

But it's also a huge opportunity for others to benefit.

As I make clear in this book, this opportunity is not all about profiting from people who have faced challenges keeping up with their mortgage payments. Often we are able to help these people more than the banks do.

It is about benefiting from the bad business decisions the banks and financial institutions made in the past... and crucially are still making.

The truth is this is something we really don't hear about on the news. It's not a common strategy when you talk to real estate investors.

In fact, most real estate investors buy and hold, or buy and flip, and that's about as sophisticated as most investors go... But if you're willing to do some work and be creative in the field, I'm going to share some strategies with you which I'm sure you will find really interesting.

WHAT IS NOTE INVESTING?

"Look at market fluctuations as your friend rather than your enemy;
profit from folly rather than participate in it."

Warren Buffett

Let's start by getting a clear understanding of what a note actually is.

If you've got something like one of the following, you have a note:

- Mortgage
- Credit card
- Car payment
- Student loan
- Second mortgage
- Boat payment

It's an IOU.

You've borrowed money from a bank to buy that asset.

Notes in Brief

A real estate note is an agreement between a borrower and a lender. It's not more complicated than that.

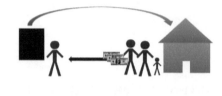

A Real Estate Note is:
- An agreement between a borrower and a lender
- Has a Principal (the loan amount owed)
- Has Interest Payments (paid monthly)

It has principal, which is just a fancy word, of course, for the loan amount which is owed.

It also has interest payments which are paid monthly.

So the occupier of the house pays the man or the woman who owns the note in exchange for being able to live in the house.

See the thing most people forget is that, if you have a mortgage on your house, you actually don't own that house. The bank does. You're making payments towards it.

One day, assuming you pay off your mortgage entirely, you will actually own your own home.

But until the loan is paid off, the bank (or whoever holds the note) owns it. It's just being held in trust for you by the bank.

So, essentially, a real estate note is an agreement between a borrower and a lender.

Buying and Selling Notes

What a lot of people don't know is that these mortgages and loans get bought and sold all the time.

Many times people will go out and get a mortgage and then a week or a month after they close, they get a letter saying that their note has been sold to a different bank.

These notes are what we invest in.

Most people think that it's big business on Wall Street trading these loans.

And, for the most part, that is true. There's a lot of Wall Street firms that buy and sell mortgages.

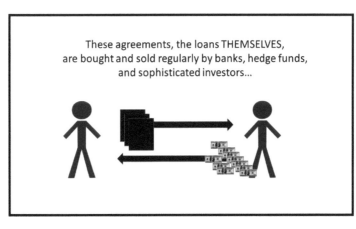

These agreements, the loans THEMSELVES, are bought and sold regularly by banks, hedge funds, and sophisticated investors...

However, most people believe that you need to have $5 million, $10 million to be playing in this game.

That used to be the case, but with everything happening in the last eight, nine years, that market has changed.

Now a secondary market has popped up for smart investors out there, that can go in and buy smaller pools or smaller tranches of these types of assets from banks and Wall Street hedge funds.

These big funds sometimes need to get some of the loans off their books and recycle their money.

This makes for a great opportunity for smart investors to come in and cherry-pick four, five, ten, 50, 100 assets if they want to.

Rehabbing the Loan

The key to understanding note investing is that instead of trying to profit by rehabbing properties... like a lot of people are used to... we actually focus on buying the debt and rehabbing the borrower.

We literally go out and buy toxic mortgages, toxic assets, from banks and hedge funds.

Then we develop some exit strategy that makes sense and is a win-win for the borrower and for us.

Now when I say "toxic assets", right away I'm sure you are thinking that's got to be extremely risky.

But the fact is the toxic element is more for the banks that made these loans.

They made these loans, they offered up 95% financing to people that had sub-par credit.

You've probably heard of the sub-prime mortgages. Banks just got greedy and made loans to people that shouldn't have had loans.

It's not that the people getting the loans were bad people. It was bad business by the banks.

The banks just got greedy.

What we are doing is buying those mortgages from banks that are securing residential commercial properties.

We then become the bank and work to create a win-win scenario with the borrowers who aren't currently making their payments.

For example, we may try to get them to start making payments, something to keep them in the property so that we have taken a nonperforming asset and turned it into a performing asset. Let me give you an example to explain this more clearly...

HOW NOTE INVESTING WORKS

"Buying real estate is not only the best way, the quickest way, the safest way, but the only way to become wealthy."

Marshall Field

Imagine you've got a borrower who owes more on their house than they can afford to pay, and then the bank isn't getting payments because the borrower's not paying their mortgage.

What the bank does, because of federal regulations, is they have to sell that loan which they've made, and get rid of it now.

That's when an investor like me or a hedge fund comes along and buys that loan for a discount.

We do that because the real estate asset on which the loan is secured is still worth something.

We'll go through some numbers to make it easier to follow.

Let's say, a few years back, a borrower went out and bought a house that was worth $150,000 and they got a $150,000 mortgage.

But then, what happened across the country? Values declined in a lot of areas.

So that $150,000 property may then only be worth $100,000.

If you're a borrower, and you're on the hook for the $150,000 mortgage that's only worth $100,000, there's not a lot of motivation to keep making your payments on time.

The value's dropped.

Other things happen:

- People get sick
- They get laid off
- There's a death in the family
- They go through a divorce

The truth is a lot of things happen to good people, financial hiccups.

For every month that a borrower does not make a payment, the face value of the mortgage starts to decline 5% to 10%.

You don't have to be a mathematician to realize that if someone goes three months, four months, five months late, that mortgage of $150,000 may be only worth $70,000 or $75,000 because the borrower's not paying on time.

The bank is upside down on the paper and they've got to get it off their books.

So we will come in and, if the house if worth $100,000 for me as an investor, *I have to buy that paper at something that makes sense for me to have a good yield.*

The Keys to Profit

There's a couple of keys to making money in note investment.

First, you want to make sure you're buying something at a discount that makes sense.

You've heard of "location, location, location," when you're buying real estate. Buying notes is all about "value, value, value."

You want to make sure that you have an accurate valuation of the asset.

If the house is worth $100,000 and you're picking up that mortgage at $40,000, it gives you a lot of room in case the air conditioner gets stolen or it needs some new plumbing, or new electrical, or new sheet rock, or new paint, or new carpet.

Buying at 40%, 50% of value gives you a lot of room.

Whereas, if you're going out and buying a foreclosure or a fix and flipper on the open market, or off the MLS, you may be in at $70,000 or $80,000, so you don't have a lot of room for mistakes.

In that case, you're paying 70% or 80% of the value, as opposed to 40% or 50% of the total actual value.

When Things Go Wrong

Here's the thing... we've bought a few houses with some holes in them, which is okay.

For example, we came across a portfolio of assets in 20 different states. You've got to check the values, so we always try to send a professional out there.

If you're buying a mortgage in Columbus, Ohio, you need to have someone go take a look at the house.

So we sent a realtor out to look at a chunk of them in Columbus, Ohio.

When you're buying in bulk, a lot of times you have a nationwide company that will pool the values for you. I prefer local people, but for the sake of time and doing our due diligence, we had to send a nationwide firm out.

This realtor, did a really good job on eleven out of twelve homes in Columbus.

They sent us pictures back of this beautiful little white siding, three-bedroom, two-bath house, about 1200 square foot. It looked perfect on the BPO (Broker's Price of Paying). It looked awesome.

But this one home, they screwed up on.

They obviously did not get out of the car to walk around the property.

We saw the photos that they sent us originally and it looked great so we bought it.

When we later drove by, there is a big hole in the side of the house that looks like Superman flew through it.

Luckily, we didn't pay a lot for the house. We literally paid $1,000 for this asset.

Even with the hole, it's worth about $25,000.

It's going to take us about ten grand to fix it but that's why we have insurance as well. Insurance is going to cover that check we have to write.

It's still going to be a profitable deal, but sometimes you have uh-ohs or ah-has along the way.

The good thing is that *if you're buying cheap enough, you're buying real estate at a big enough discount, you can afford these issues once in a while.*

Of course, you don't want to be making mistakes like this, but it's not a death sentence because our risk is really mitigated and spread out over multiple assets.

That's why we try to buy in bulk. I picked up five properties in Florida recently worth $330,000. I picked them up for just under $99,000, really decent properties.

Within the first three weeks, three of the borrowers are willing to modify their loans to us, which will end up equating roughly to about a 29% yield to us on those.

The other two we'll foreclose, and then make some really nice profits by selling the assets off as REOs at full market value.

What We Look For

So when we're buying notes, what do we look for specifically in these types of assets?

My biggest thing is I like occupied assets. I want to keep the borrowers in the properties because, not only is it a good thing, the property's probably in better shape than if it was vacant and less chance for it to be vandalized.

There are a lot more exit strategies to deal with when I'm working with an occupied asset.

There's government programs where states and the government will pay me money to modify the loans, in roughly 19 states across the country. It's something called the hardship funds.

If we can modify the loan, it also gives me a lot of flexibility to start having money come in immediately, versus if it's vacant, then I've got to start the foreclosure process. I've got to do rehab.

Foreclosure process can take anywhere from 30 days, in Texas and Georgia, all the way up to three years, if you're investing in New York.

I like looking at owner occupied assets in faster foreclosure states where the values have started to come back, like Florida. Florida may be nine to 12 months to foreclose, it's got a lot of appreciation. There's a lot of people moving to Florida.

I also like Indiana. Great mortgage recovery. It's also fast to evict in Indiana.

I like North Carolina, South Carolina. Values are coming back strong there. There's a lot of great markets out there.

Some people are scared of Detroit because of what happened there. Detroit has been on sale for years and they're one of the strongest appreciating markets out there right now, averaging 23% appreciation the last four years.

I look for where people are going to go. I look for major universities. Those are the biggest things that I look for.

We also have to double check taxes because if somebody's not paying their mortgage payment for four years, they're obviously not paying their taxes.

That's the second thing besides checking value and occupancy that we're going to check is how much is owed in taxes, and make sure that a tax foreclosure hasn't wiped us out.

Scope of the Market

Think about how many trillions of dollars of real estate there is in the United States alone. Then you look at *almost every piece of real estate is going to have some sort of mortgage on it.*

Most real estate is not owned cash. Some is, a very small percentage, but most people have a mortgage of some kind on it. They're making payments every month to a bank, so to speak, but the bank isn't always the bank.

This is the dirty little secret. The bank could be a person. If I own a home, and I sell it to you and I say, "Hey, I'll finance this house to you," now I've become the bank.

We make a little loan agreement, called a note, and you make your payments every month to me and now I'm the so-called bank.

There's some regulation that requires that you do this and not that, and you charge a certain interest rate or what have you, but the interesting thing is there's a lot of people out there who are actually acting like the bank.

I'm one of those people and what I'm doing is I'm going to banks, which specialize in creating these loans, because when you need a loan the bank is the one that creates loans.

They create mortgages, and then they sell them off. Typically, they'll sell them off to Wall Street when they're doing well, and they're performing, and everyone's making their payments, and everything's peachy.

When things aren't going well, and there's five, 10, 15, 100, 200, 500 loans that a bank owns where the borrower is not making their payments, where that's happening, those loans get taken off to the side and then sold off to investors, who are willing to pay basically to go fix the problem.

The bank doesn't want to fix the problem. The bank just wants to create more loans, because they get paid when they create their loans and when they sell their loans.

It's called getting their loans off the books.

What happens is hedge funds and private investors, high net worth individuals, come along and buy that loan that's delinquent, where that borrower's not been making their payments for seven, eight, 10, 12, 36 months.

Basically, we buy it at a 50%, 60%, 70% discount to what the real estate is worth.

That's the key, because every mortgage is secured by the real estate and if you don't pay, it's just a matter of time before the bank can take the real estate.

In this case, I am the bank. If you don't pay, you don't stay.

The idea is that, in some states, it will take a long time to get the borrower out of the house so that you can sell the house or get someone in there who can pay. In other states, you can do it really quickly.

That's where the game is, in figuring out which states to invest in, and which borrowers you should go after and which ones you shouldn't, and which ones you should try to keep in their home, and which ones are basically degenerates and just need to be kicked to the curb.

The old ladies, the people who are working hard and are just on tough times, but are willing to work with you and make an honest effort to stay in their homes, those are the ones that are like gold.

You work with them, they want to stay in their house, you want to keep them in their house, and you can work with that and you can make money.

The idea here is that by buying notes, by buying these nonperforming notes... meaning mortgages that are not current, that are past due where the borrower hasn't paid in some time... you can go in there, buy it at a huge discount, and work with that borrower or get that borrower out of the house, then own that asset or control that asset and be able to make a 15%, 20%, 30% yield.

Whereas if you just bought a house that's an investment property, maybe you're earning 6% or 8%.

By going out and buying these nonperforming notes, we are able to get all this real estate at a huge discount and, as a result of that, be able to build a huge amount of wealth and great cash flow.

That's the big thing is we try to get them performing and it becomes cash flow.

Landlords like mailbox money. I like bank money, where it gets wired directly to my account with the payments that these borrowers are making monthly.

THE PROFIT PROCESS

"Landlords grow rich in their sleep without working, risking or economizing."

John Stuart Mill

Let me talk a little about how we make money in the notes business, because it's not like we are buying a house for $100,000 and then selling it for $150,000, which everybody can understand.

Perhaps it works best if I give you a deal example.

We picked up this mortgage. Borrower owed $130,000 on their house. It was in Cape Coral, Florida.

When we got the mortgage sent to us, we were reevaluating the deal. The house was worth about $95,000, so they were upside down by about $40,000. In other words, they owed $40,000 more than the house was worth.

The borrower had not made a payment in three plus years and they were still living in the house.

We ended up negotiating with the hedge fund to buy that mortgage at $45,000, about 50% of the value.

- We bought the mortgage, which hadn't been paid in three years, for $45,000

- The house is worth $90,000

- They owe $130,000 on it and some change

- We literally picked the mortgage up for about 35% of what was owed, 50% of value

Florida is a little bit longer foreclosure process. That's why we got it at such a good price, as well.

We reached out to the borrower, "We'd like to offer you a modification." They wouldn't return our phone calls. Wouldn't return our letters.

A modification just basically says we want to work with you to get you making payments now. It's something similar to rent, "Your mortgage payment was $1200, let's have you make a payment of about $800," which was market rent in the same area.

They wouldn't respond. We're literally going through the foreclosure process, a nine-month process. The borrower shows up right before foreclosure, "Oh, I want to stay in the house now, but I only want to make a $500 a month payment."

I'm like, "No offense, you've had your opportunity." We've had these foreclosure costs. We've had these attorneys along the way.

The asset now, over that nine-month period, has appreciated. It's gone from being worth $90,000 to $130,000 now. We just had another $35,000 to $40,000 in appreciation.

We would have been glad to modify that loan, or the payments with the borrower on the front end. Since they weren't willing to work with us, we don't run a charity. You're not going to stay for free.

We ended up finishing the foreclosure process and we even went to the borrower and told her, "We're foreclosing on you. We're going to give you $1000, though, to move out and leave the property in good condition."

It's well worth $1000 to make sure that they didn't trash the property. Little incentives like that.

So she did. She moved out, left the property in good condition. That $1000 helped her pay her deposit wherever she was going, or pay some bills. It allowed us, too, to take the property back with less repairs.

We were able to market the property faster and get a full price offer at $129,900 within 48 hours of listing it on the MLS.

Simple Process

So we bought the property for $45,000, foreclosed on it, which we basically had an attorney do all that. We had servicing companies. There's vendors out there that handle everything.

There's a whole list of vendors that have popped up that will either service your loan, whether you've got one loan or 1000 loans, foreclosure attorneys in every state that it's their job to handle the foreclosure.

- We bought this property for $45,000 by buying the note behind the property

- We foreclosed on it, and then were able to sell it for about $130,000 with $15,000 of closing costs

- We ended up netting $115,000 after closing costs, so it's a $70,000 profit.

That took nine months and that's a 100% return. Over 100% yield on our money.

Again, investors are out there beating their heads against the wall, trying to get 8% on their money.

You go into Nashville, for example, you try to buy an investment property right now, you're lucky if you can get a 7% return.

You buy a property for $100,000, you get $7,000 a year in cash flow. That's as good as it gets when you're buying a rental property.

We have properties that turn into rental properties. We could have kept this property and turned around and rented it out for $900 a month if we wanted to.

- We bought it for $45,000

- We could rent it for $900 a month

- So we're making like a 20% return a year

It's all because we're buying so cheap.

There's a whole variety of different exit strategies. Yes, we do foreclose. Yes, we do end up selling some of these assets off. Sometimes we'll pay the borrower money just to walk.

That's called cash for keys.

If the borrower can't make a payment that makes sense, they don't want to stay in the property, we'll literally sometimes just ask the borrower to give us the property back.

In some cases, when we do have to give money, we'll incentivize the borrower $1000, $500, $10,000. Just give us the keys, we'll let you walk. Don't fight us, because we're going to end up winning it in the foreclosure trial. Just walk.

You make your money in real estate on the buy, and that's what everybody knows and says. You make your money when you buy.

Of course, if markets go up or down, whatever, if you buy cheap enough, over the long term, unless there's some sort of long term crash which nobody could foresee, you make your money on the buy. *If you buy cheap enough, you make money.*

WHY THE BANKS SELL

"Real estate cannot be lost or stolen, nor can it be carried away. Purchased with common sense, paid for in full, and managed with reasonable care, it is about the safest investment in the world."

Franklin D. Roosevelt

So what are the reasons that a bank doesn't work with a borrower the way that I would work with a borrower?

Let's say a bank has a bad mortgage; they've got a borrower who hasn't made a payment on a loan in seven months, eight months.

The first thing is, banks are very heavily regulated.

They must actually write off their bad debts periodically or they become insolvent and might have to shut down and go out of business completely; something which they clearly will avoid at all costs, especially since they're using other people's money, not their own.

You might wonder why wouldn't they just go in and try to work with the borrower and get them paying, or buy them out of the house and say, "Listen, I'll give you five grand. You go away. I'll sell the house. We'll call it even."

Well the truth is that some banks will do it, but they're not really good at it.

The thing that you have to realize when you have a large bank out there, they're hiring employees and the employees don't have a vested interest in the successful outcome, or helping the borrower one way or another.

They're just interested in keeping their job. They're getting paid $15 an hour, $20 an hour. They don't really care.

They're not high level employees and they've got a stack of 500 mortgages on their table. You just become a number.

Then the federal regulations are such that banks aren't allowed to keep these nonperforming loans on their books, so to speak, for a long period of time because it prevents them from doing more loans.

Their business is writing and creating more new loans, it's not fixing the small percentage of bad loans that they do have. So they just want to get rid of them.

In a lot of cases they do, but also a lot of the time, if they make a loan for $150,000 and the house is now worth $100,000, they don't want to have that on their books, unless it's federally insured or they've got some sort of bailout.

You have to realize, banks are leveraging every dollar that is on deposit, somewhere between five, 10, 15 times what is in the deposit.

Literally, they're making loans out and leveraging all this money. It's not good for them to start taking write downs. If I'm the bank, and I make a loan for $150,000 and I created that mortgage, I don't really want to modify the loan and forgive principal.

We've made a loan for $150,000, we've got to write it down to $75,000, ugh, it's tough. They don't want to do that. They'd rather sell it off, take it as a write off on their books, and it becomes a win-win for everyone.

Pooling Together

If you go to a hedge fund buying 1000 of these nonperforming, or basically just delinquent mortgages, people who've not paid their mortgage in a long time, the bank will pool all of these together.

If there's 50 in Detroit, and 100 in California, and 55 in Florida, the bank maybe has all of these and they put them all together and they sell them out as a package.

Sometimes they sell in a package. Sometimes they'll let you cherry pick. It just depends on the situation.

So a bank may sell a big package to a hedge fund and then you may go to the hedge fund and then get five, six, seven, eight, ten assets out of there.

Recently, Fanny Mae sold 3700 mortgages to a firm out of Dallas. That firm has an ideal property type that they like to control, three-bedroom, two-bath, built after 2001, 1500+ square foot.

There's a lot of mortgages in that large bundle where the property that is securing it does not match that, so they want to move those off of their books.

Out of that 3700, they may be selling off half of that to investors like myself in smart pools. We're not buying 3700 mortgages, but we're buying 50, or 20, or 10, depending on the situation. It's kind of trickle-down economics. Ross Perot will be proud, I guess.

- Someone's buying 3700 from a bigger bank

- That 3700 may get divvied up into six pools of about 600 buyers

- One of those hedge funds has bought 600 and they keep 300

- They then sell another 300 off to a smaller firm like myself

We've been so successful at this that we're actually starting a hedge fund now to be able to take money in to invest for people who want to do this.

We've been really toying with that idea for a while. I've closed on over a half billion dollars in note deals since 2007.

It just makes sense. We're buying in bigger pools. We have a lot of bigger sources coming to us, so it makes it easier for us to convert inverse investments and inverse asset funds into a hedge fund, and get it approved by the FCC and go from there.

THE COMING MORTGAGE MELTDOWN

"If you don't own a home, buy one. If you own a home, buy another one. If you own two homes, buy a third. And, lend your relatives the money to buy a home."

John Paulson

You might be wondering why aren't people doing this? Why don't people know about this?

It's just a niche. There's not many people that teach it across the country. Very, very few people know about it. A lot of people fall in love with the TV shows: "Flip this Rock," or "Flip this Shack."

They love the idea of picking out paint colors and carpet. I don't like that stuff. I want to make money. I'm an ROI based investor. That's one thing that unites all of us real estate investors is what's your return on investment? What do your paychecks look like?

Unfortunately, *a lot of investors, they pay too much for their properties that they're going to fix and flip.*

They want to feel like they're doing a deal. But, if they start calculating their ROIs on their paper, they're losing money, or they're getting paid less than what McDonald's are paying their employees, which they figure out.

Many people buy properties and renovate them, and at the end of the day, sell them. However,

- By the time you pay the real estate broker

- By the time you pay the title company

- By the time you pay everybody who's got their hand out wanting to get money

... you make a few thousand dollars, but you spent 200 hours managing contractors, going to the site, picking paint colors, all these things.

You end up making a few thousand dollars, and it's really not worth the risk, though, and the time for most people.

People think, "Hey, I closed the deal. That's awesome." Most people don't think on it as an investor basis. They don't think, "What's my time worth? What's my money worth?"

That's the most important aspect of it. I want to be swimming and fishing in the biggest pools. A lot of real estate investors are used to mailing out postcards to people that are losing their homes, trying to get that one property.

Me, I don't want to go after one borrower who owns one property. I want to go for the bank who's got hundreds and thousands of deals that I can cherry-pick and tap into, and avoid a lot of the drama that most traditional investors have.

The Big Opportunity

To understand why note investing offers such a huge opportunity, we need to take a step back in time.

Literally five years ago, a lot of banks were modifying loans by just taking the interest rate and dropping it from 8% or 6% to 2%, and they were doing five-year fixed rates at 1% or 2%.

What's happened now is that five-year period has expired, and so the loans are starting to adjust back up to 5%, 6%, 7%.

Banks were hoping that the values would come back from $100,000 to $150,000 over that five-year time frame, but that's not been the case in a lot of markets.

In some cases, it has but what's unfortunate is you've got a borrower in the property now who's used to a 2% interest rate, and now they can't afford a 6% interest rate. Their mortgage payment tripled.

Now you've had somebody that's lived in a house for two, three, four, five years, a good borrower, but just is not budget mindful that their payments are going to change, and now they're in default again. It's the whole same thing all over again like it was seven years ago.

Mortgage Meltdown

Basically, all of the loan modifications and the government bailouts that happened five years ago have created a period of stability, but *the period of stability is coming to an end* because most of these mortgages weren't modified indefinitely.

As the markets declined across the country and we had the first Mortgage Meltdown in 2007, 2008 and 2009, there were literally 15 million homes, 15 million borrowers, where they owed more on their houses than their properties were worth.

The beautiful thing about that is these banks, once these loans started nonperforming, they could not hold on to them.

The paper was not worth what the property was worth. So they have to sell these assets off at huge discounts to other investors like me.

And they had to sell at a big discount to incentivize us to take over their nightmares.

The fact is that we could pick up this debt at a fraction of what is owed and that gives us a lot of flexibility to create good situations to keep the borrowers in their homes.

You've got this Mortgage Meltdown 2.0 coming because you've got all these loans, which everyone thinks are safe and doing well and doing fine right now, that are about to reset to a much higher rate.

The reason we had the first Mortgage Meltdown was the adjustable rate mortgages, partly, and when those reset or those increased, people couldn't afford their loans anymore.

They can barely afford the houses they're in now.

You've got all these mortgages that are about to come to the market as nonperforming, meaning delinquent or late, and so that presents a huge opportunity.

There's another three to five million modified loans out there that are going to reset over the next three to five years.

There are still seven million delinquent from the original Mortgage Meltdown and another five million coming.

It's almost a doubling of the amount of nonperforming notes out there.

All Over Again

Plus, then you start looking at what Wall Street and the banks are starting to do with sub-prime coming back, and starting to make risky loans again. It's history repeating itself.

People tend to think everything just went fine after the last crisis. With the bailout, things stabilized. So we think, "Oh, it wasn't that bad. We can do the same thing again. It'll all work out. It worked out last time."

During the peak, JPMorgan Chase was leveraged about ten to one. They're currently, in today's market, leveraged across the world, leveraged about 50 to one.

It's a worse leverage position than it was back eight, nine years ago, and that's just JPMorgan Chase. A lot of the other banks are at that. It's mind-numbingly scary that we're going to see another meltdown again.

We're already seeing it on the commercial side in different markets. It's a huge opportunity if you know where to be playing, but what's also scary is you have a lot of investors who've gone out and bought property, have paid 70, 80 cents of value, to be landlords.

You May Be Wondering
How Many of These Loans Are There Out There?

$137,658,158,000

Distressed Single Family Assets at U.S. Banks

DistressedPro.com

They want to get some cash flow. What's going to happen to their deals, or their properties, when the market drops 10%, 20%, 30%? They're also going to start to be underwater.

They don't have the leverage like I do. If I'm at 40% of value and the market drops 30%, I've still got 30% in the black, not in the red.

I've got a lot of flexibility to be able to keep somebody in that property, adjust their payment down, and work with them to create a win-win still.

HOW TO BENEFIT FROM THE NOTE INVESTING OPPORTUNITY

"This is a real-estate-driven economy from top to bottom."

Christopher Thornberg

I teach people how to do note investing so that they can follow in our footsteps and make money as an investor, or even as full-time job if they want to be doing this.

Why I Share My Knowledge

Let me talk a little bit about why I do that. Why I spend some of my time training and educating people when I'm building a hedge fund and I do these deals all the time on my own.

When I started off in 2007, it was a very, very niche market. Very, very few people knew how to buy notes.

I was having success buying one-offs, but it wasn't the easiest thing to raise capital. I had people that were interested in funding our deals, but they wanted to know more about it, so teaching just became a natural side product of it.

It was just a function of raising money and developing a nationwide network of investors that I could reach out to, to either help me perform due diligence and drive by the properties, or potential buyers for the pools that I was buying and the assets I didn't want to keep myself.

I could build a bigger buyer's list so that instead of me buying five, I could buy 50. Instead of buying 50, I could buy 150.

It's like Costco. You get a bulk package. You get a better pricing than if you're buying just one note.

So *there is an incentive to have a lot of people in my network,* in my group, buying these note deals because I then get a bigger and bigger discount the more people that buy these notes.

The more they're buying, the bigger discounts we get, the better deals we get, the better pricing we get on servicing and our vendors. So it becomes a true win-win across the board.

I closed on over 700 assets in 2015. We expect to close on over 1000 deals in 2016.

In terms of my own financial situation, we're sitting pretty well. I own, currently, 300 plus assets across the country. A large chunk of those are performing or turned into rentals that we keep for cash flow.

That's what I do first and foremost is buy assets for my own portfolio and teach other people how to do them. It's become a passion because there's literally like 4500 lending institutions out there with bad paper.

There are still almost eight million homes under water across the United States, so there's a huge pool to fish in. I can't buy them all.

I wish I could. Someday, maybe, we'll see how it goes.

Literally, we really, truly are changing America one mortgage at a time because we are buying in bulk, really helping not only the borrowers out but the communities out by avoiding foreclosures hitting the market.

We're keeping values up because they're not being listed and being sold and long list times.

We're really giving these borrowers back their dream of home ownership and taking a nightmare and turning it back into a dream for them.

Loving What I Do

I love what I do. I absolutely love getting up each day. I love talking with my attorneys on what's going on. I love talking with the servicing company.

I love the fact that I get stories like Sheila in South Beloit, Illinois, who was in her house for 18 years, and her husband got sick. They were four years behind, and they'd been trying to do the loan modification for four years, and turned down, and turned down, and turned down.

Then we got her mortgage. We reached out to her.

She wants to stay in the property. She's got five grand that she's been saving to put towards the loan right now. She can make a normal mortgage payment, and it's a true win-win scenario for her.

That's one of the great things. I love helping people. I love seeing the light go off in new investors' eyes, and them walk with a little bit more of an upright and shoulders back and really proud because they're going out and closing deals, and making money in real estate for the first time ever.

They're changing their way. They're able to leave that J-O-B that they hate. Those are the most exciting things about what I do. I absolutely love that. Yes, we make great money, but *we make great money by helping other people make money.* That's the most important thing.

They stay in their house. They're not having to move out. They're not having to try to find an apartment complex.

Most of the time, it's cheaper for borrowers to work with me. If they were to move out, they're going to have to pay the first and last month's rent. They're going to get deposits for the electrical. They're going to have to move. They're going to uproot their kids to new school districts.

The embarrassment of telling their family or friends, "I've got to move out because we're losing the house," that's devastating, not only to an ego, but to a family, a marriage, a lot of times. It's totally devastating.

Whereas, listen, that three grand to five grand that you would be paying to move, pay it to me towards your mortgage.

Let's work out a situation, and really help you reset your life, resuscitate that dream, and take something bad in a bad situation and turn it into something.

It's kind of like the tagline for inverse investments is turning problem properties into profitable solutions.

THE NOTE BUYING BLUEPRINT: YOUR STEP-BY-STEP GUIDE

"Real estate is an imperishable asset, ever increasing in value. It is the most solid security that human ingenuity has devised. It is the basis of all security and about the only indestructible security."

Russell Sage

I've seen a lot of real estate investors that go from workshop to workshop, class to class, and pay all this money and they don't have really any type of game plan, any type of blueprint to help them go from where they're at today to success tomorrow.

That's why we've created the Note Buying Blueprint - Note Genius Suite. It's literally a step-by-step game plan for you to really accomplish and become a true note investor, really become an investor and not a pretender (get a special offer for the Note Genius Suite at the end of the chapter).

The first thing we start off with is we try to put you through a three-day workshop. It's called my Note Buying for Dummies workshop.

It's literally three days of content, of us going through the nuts and bolts, the A-Z process of buying notes.

We focus on the three Fs of note buying: How to Find, Fund, and then Flip.

Flip stands for a lot of different exit strategies we can do, so that we can focus on the three Fs of the note buying. That's the first thing.

You got to have a good foundation, good basic knowledge before you're able to run. We'll get you crawling in that aspect of that.

Then we also throw in some really great bonuses along the way with that.

- **30-day Note Training Series:** This is basically a video for the first 30 days, along with an email straight to your inbox, giving you now that you've gone through the workshop, this is what you need to do Day One; this is what you need to do Day Two, Day Three, Day Four. Here's the things you've got to keep in mind to really get you up and running.

- **30-day Marketing Training Series:** The next thing we go through is where really a lot of investors, especially new investors who are leaving their job or leaving a career to get into this, struggle with, and that's marketing.

So we've got a 30-day marketing series that my buddy Chase Thompson, who's a marketing guru, put together to help us out with that.

You've got 30-day note training, 30-day marketing, to really help you get rock and rolling, and that leads into the biggest thing that a lot of investors have a headache with, is the funding side.

- **30-Day Private Capital Raising Series:** With note investing, you've got to have cash to buy assets. You can't go to a bank to get a loan. It just doesn't work. You've got to have cash.

But don't flip out if you don't have cash. There's literally seven trillion dollars in private money sitting out there. Seven trillion dollars not making anything, really losing money.

We show you, with our third bonus, my 30-day private capital raising series, which is so awesome. Literally, people love this training.

It's actually how I raised money. I gave you sample deals. I gave you sample contracts, sample forms. We literally give you scripts. We give you investor profile sheets. We give you examples and solutions to the questions people are going to ask. We show you how to interview private investors. We show you how to raise that over a 30-day period.

Those are the three big bonuses. You also get the amazing Note Buying Blueprint home study course that we've put together.

You're getting five things in the Note Buying Blueprint – Note Genius Suite:

- Virtual Note Buying for Dummies
- 30-Day Note Training
- 30-Day Marketing Training
- 30-Day Raising Private Capital
- Note Buying Blueprint Home Study Course Training

The actual Note Blueprint itself walks you through step-by-step, literally, where you go online to research buying notes; how you find asset managers who have these notes to sell; what you say to the asset manager in order for them to take you seriously and avoid sounding like everyone else who's calling them.

Again, more strategies for getting your deals closed and funded, and who you should you work with; what servicing companies you need; what mistakes you should avoid; what you should say, what you should not say.

There's so much great information in this training, that literally in a 30-day period, you could become a yellow belt, and then in another 30 days, you could become a brown belt, and then within 90 days you could become, literally, a note black belt by doing all of these various different trainings, these three 30-day trainings, plus the Note Buying Blueprint itself.

Again, you've got to have this training in order to be able to do this. This is a specialty. This is a niche within a niche.

This is real estate investing by buying mortgages, and it's not what everyone does, it's not what everyone knows how to do, and it's very different than just going out and buying a piece of real estate. It's totally different.

Ready to become a Note Genius? Go to
https://notebuyingblueprint.com/book

Becoming King of the Hill

The cool thing is that it's secured by the real estate. In fact, when you look at the whole landscape of real estate, and you look at the whole hierarchy, meaning who's the king, who's the prince, who's the pauper?

In this whole setup, the king is the person at the top of the pyramid, and guess who that is? That's the bank, and you can be the bank. You can be the one who has the claim on the real estate.

People think that they own their own homes. You do if you paid cash for it, and you're on the deed and nobody else is on the deed, and you own it.

If you have a mortgage on your house, the bank owns it. They own it in trust for you. They're holding it for you, but they own it. If you stop making the payments, they take away what belongs to them, essentially.

You can have that position in the real estate investing. We call that going upstream, meaning everybody else is downstream fighting over the crumbs, and *you can go upstream to the top of the pyramid and basically be the king of the hill by being the bank.*

It requires that you change your viewpoint. It requires that you change your perspective a little bit in how you're going to do the real estate and that you don't fall in love with having to be the one that's picking out the paint colors, and picking up the hammer, and bossing around contractors, and real busy, busy, busy bees. It's easier to make money than it is to be busy, in my opinion.

Most investors struggle because they're too busy being control freaks about picking everything and managing people.

Me, I want to put systems in place, I want to manage my vendors, and manage my systems. That's how you become wealthy, no matter what you do.

You have systems in place and you manage the vendors.

That's how Henry Ford became wealthy. It's how all the entrepreneurs out there that are successful became successful. They put systems in place and they don't have to manage the people.

The systems manage the people, and that's what I show you in the Note Buying Blueprint.

The little things in note investing, it can be a little overwhelming sometimes, but that's why we give you these extra bonuses in the Note Genius Suite, to really help guide you on the right path to real estate success.

Elite Mastermind

The good thing is that you're not alone in this. There's other people. I have an elite group of people in my mastermind, who pay about $10,000 a year to come together in either Austin, Texas, or Hawaii, or wherever it is in the world that they want to go do this thing.

In fact, we've just been to Puerto Rico as a group because we had a bank that gave us 500 assets to look at in Puerto Rico.

So we do this at a very, very high level. If you're a very serious investor, if you're someone who's done a ton of deals, you may want to skip this whole thing and just go straight into the Mastermind.

While I could say that that's okay, I'm actually going to tell you it's not.

You need to know the fundamentals. If you just show up to the mastermind with a bunch of cash, you're going to look like an idiot.

And we actually won't let anybody do that.

So even if you have the cash to play the big leagues and get access to me personally, to get access to my top guys who are making $100,000 a year, $200,000 a year, $300,000 a year, buying and selling and trading notes... even if you could pay that and that made sense for you... we would still encourage you to go through the training and get all of the training step-by-step.

Because otherwise you're not going to understand what the questions are to ask.

You won't understand where you should be investing, which states are good, which states aren't good, what kinds of assets, how big of an asset should you buy?

There's all these questions that really need to get answered and there are correct answers to these questions.

We usually start buying mortgages on assets at $200,000 of value for the property or less. We have bought some million dollar mortgages and things like that in the residential side. They have a tendency to drag out.

Ninety-five percent of the mortgages that are in trouble are the mortgages backing $200,000 assets or less.

Think about that. $200,000 might buy you a dog house in California, but it might buy you a mansion in Columbus, Ohio. We stay in that lower end.

There's a lot more strategies, a lot more borrowers, a lot more buyers in case we end up having to sell the asset. That's the biggest thing.

SO... if you're ready to start buying these real estate assets in a smart way, in a profitable way, in the note way, become an investor with us by picking up the Note Buying Blueprint – Note Genius Suite today. Go to https://notebuyingblueprint.com/book for the complete package at over 50% off the normal price and get all of the bonuses included FREE.

HELPING PEOPLE AND THE WINDOW OF OPPORTUNITY

"Before you start trying to work out which direction the property market is headed, you should be aware that there are markets within markets."

Paul Clitheroe

Unfortunately, the United States is good at creating a lot of poor people, and so we try to work with that market to help make housing affordable for them, to really keep them in their properties.

If they're willing to help themselves a lot of times, to create a situation that is beneficial to them to stay, versus being out on the streets and not knowing where they have to go next, then we can create a win-win.

There's a lot of really good people out there. There's a lot of hard-working people who don't make a huge income every year.

They're living in middle class or lower middle class neighborhoods. They're safe neighborhoods.

They're neighborhoods where people care about what's happening, and those are great neighborhoods to invest in, as opposed to the $300,000, $400,000, $500,000 homes where, frankly, someone is about to lose that kind of home, they probably have equity. They put down 20% on a house like that.

They're also going to fight you. They're going to have their attorney. They're going to pay the $1,500 to their attorney a month to drag the foreclosure out, versus paying the $5,000 or $4,000 a month payment to you.

This isn't taking advantage of poor people. That's not a good business, and we do not do that. We want to work to create a win-win scenario; a win for our borrowers and a win for us.

If any situation, any business deal, or any type of deal, is only a win on one party's side, it's not a good scenario. That's the big thing we want to do. We want to help people out.

We want to keep people in their homes, but we also want to make money.

There is plenty of opportunity out there. Seven to ten million homes, seven to ten million opportunities, for you to do just that in itself.

I would say there's less than probably 5,000 true note investors across the country. Think about that.

There's a lot more fix and flippers. I ran out of fingers and toes a long time ago on that. I would say if I had to venture a guess, it's probably 125,000 to 150,000.

You figure that's 5,000 versus 125,000. That is a lot less competition.

Twenty-five times the competition when you buy a fix and flip, versus when you buy a note.

Sooner or later, the word is going to get out there, people are going to be getting and entering this market, and the competition will get more and more fierce.

Right now, there's a window of opportunity coming, because these mortgages are resetting.

It's the perfect storm of increasing prices, but also increasing defaults because people can't afford the increase in mortgage payments that's going to come when their mortgage is reset.

You've got rising markets, rising prices, and more and more people defaulting. It's a perfect storm for a note investor.

Brief Window of Opportunity

You have a window of opportunity here that's literally no more than three to six months before the feeding frenzy begins, and when you come to the party, you're going to be late.

As it is, you're already a little bit late to the party because the best deals are starting to hit right now.

By waiting a year, two years, and three years, and thinking about this, thinking about getting started in note investing, all that's going to do is basically have you miss out on making money.

Those people who take risks in life are the ones that do well. The days of being able to just invest your money in the bond market and the stock market, and do something that's safe and have a happy retirement, I'm sorry, but those days are long gone.

It's a rigged game anyway, and I don't want to put my money in the stock market.

I don't have any money in the stock market, because I can't control anything about it. I don't know enough. There's people who control those markets. It just came out the other day that the price of gold is being fixed. It came out that the price of this is being fixed, and that's rigged, and options are backdating.

Oil's down. You can't count on any of these things.

All you can count on is your own ingenuity, your own hard work, and that's what made America great, and that's what always made America great, and that's what will continue to make America great, and that's what will get us out of any recession or any down, difficult times which, unfortunately, are probably coming.

That's what's going to get us through. The interesting thing about the note business is it's counter-cyclical, which means that as the economy gets worse, the opportunities to make money in note investing actually get better.

This is a great, great insurance policy against a declining economy.

Just look at the writing on the wall with economic growth slowing and all this debt stuff happening in Europe, and all these economic problems that we've got.

We do have a strong housing market, but who knows how long that's going to last.

The best thing you can do to protect yourself and to protect your family from any kind of fallout that could happen from this economic decline in this next cycle that we're coming into here shortly, the best thing you can do to prepare them is to have a note investing strategy in place.

That's going to allow you to make money when everyone else is losing money, and that is so important to your survival and to the survival of your family that it's something you should really, really think about.

You can sit on the sidelines and say, "Gosh, I don't know. This is kind of risky. This is a lot of money for me to get started training on this."

You know what? It's not. What costs a lot of money is not doing anything. That's the biggest cost of anyone's life is the opportunities that they don't take.

The only thing you guarantee by not trying something is failure. That's the only thing you're ever going to guarantee is failure if you don't ever act on things.

Special Opportunity

We have a special opportunity for you today to be able to invest in this training at a huge discount. We hope you'll take us up on this.

We have put a tremendous amount of work and time into putting together all of the templates, all of the tools, all of the letters, all of the things that you're going to need in order to get started in the note business, and to be successful.

We're giving you step-by-step training on exactly how to do this, giving you access to other people, Facebook groups of like-minded individuals which you'll have access to, other people who are getting started in the note business.

You've got very sophisticated investors who've done commercial real estate, residential real estate, hotels, all these different types of investment groups, all moving out of those and into the note business.

You know when those smart investors are moving into the note business that you're even a little bit late to the party right now as it is.

The opportunity and the window is still open, though, so you've got to go. You've got to move. You've got to hustle.

Time is of the essence. You can't be trying to learn how to do this and figure this out when there's blood on the streets, and everyone is gobbling up these mortgages at huge discounts, and you miss your

There are Thousands of Banks Out There Who Have These "Toxic Assets" On Their Books

4,542

Number of Banks with Residential Loan Trouble
DistressedPro.com

But They're Really **Not Toxic**
Because They're SECURED by Properties
That are Worth Much More than the Note Itself

opportunity because you weren't prepared.

Being prepared is the key to being successful, and you need to be prepared for the Mortgage Meltdown that is coming ... I'm not trying to scare you and I don't want to be a Doomsayer, but there's going to be some economic difficulty in the next three, six, 12 months.

How prepared are you for that? How prepared are you if you were to lose your job? How prepared are you if your investment property, they weren't making their payment, they stopped paying their loans?

You see? Being prepared and having the tools and strategies in place to be able to make a 20%, 30% return, if you're smart, if you buy the assets correctly.

I can't promise you you're going to make any kind of money doing this. I can only show you the way. I can show you the door.

We really hope you take advantage of this opportunity today and that you get started, and you apply yourself diligently to learning this industry and achieving the results that are possible that are right there for you. People from all backgrounds have bought notes successfully with us. We know you can too. Go to https://notebuyingblueprint.com/book to get the Note Buying Blueprint – Note Genius Suite and join our family of like-minded note investors.

We hope you don't regret failing to take action and kick yourself 12, 16, 24 months from now when all these people are making money doing this and you're not.

Special Notice: How Your Participation Helps a Veteran

I'm a huge fan of our past and present military. They've given a lot.

They've sacrificed a lot more than most of us have, for us to be able to live in still the best country in the world.

We've got a big, big heart to help veterans out. We've got family, friends that have served in the military.

For everybody that pays to be a part of the Note Buying Blueprint program, we end up donating a free pass to a past or present military person, to give them an opportunity to start on their second career path; give them a helping hand to find some sort of success in real estate if that's the path that they choose to go.

I'm always a big believer that military can take directions. They're very coachable. They're good at following a plan of action, and we find that a lot of the military are really smart and mostly successful students.

So if you were to enroll in the Note Genius Suite today, you would be helping a member, or former member, of the armed forces get basically access to this incredible training which you're going to get access to.

That allows them to help their family and, frankly, be able to create wealth and security for their family.

That is important because they've served our country, they've secured our freedom, they've made it possible for us to enjoy this amazing opportunity, which is the note business.

That's what great about the United States. Our lending laws allow us to do this. This doesn't happen in most countries across the world. Very, very few countries have the same type of lending laws that the US has.

With what's going on now, you have got a huge opportunity in this niche.

As we all know, the riches are in the niches, and this is one of the hottest niches out there right now because it's an untapped market.

We've literally got access to seven to ten million homes, and we help a lot of military.

If one of our borrowers is a military, we bend over backwards to make sure to keep them in the property, and really create a win-win to help them out.

Back to our foundation is that our goal is to help a ton of military personnel who are getting out of the service, who are looking for a new career path; give them an opportunity to make some real money and still have a lot of freedom with being a real estate investor.

I was fortunate enough, when I graduated high school, I had a scholarship. If I hadn't had a scholarship, I'd have been going into the Marines.

I've had friends that have gone into it. I've lost friends in the different wars. I've come across a lot of people that have struggled, that are looking for something new.

They don't have that structure like they did in the military. They just need a game plan.

They need somebody to show them the way, and I'm glad to help show them that because they're going to go out and accomplish far greater things, be able to really have a dream that they can chase, have a dream that is actually attainable if they do the simple things and follow the instructions I teach in my training.

This note business is such an incredible opportunity for anybody, first of all, but to give this to our military, our armed forces, is such a gift because they're so deserving of a great opportunity.

Anyone who's a good person is deserving of a great opportunity, but particularly them because they deserve this.

This is sort of a lucky break for a lot of the military that we help through this program, and I'm incredibly passionate about this.

For each person that enrolls in our training, that's one person who's helped and who's given an opportunity to totally transform their family, and their kids, and help their wife or their husband, or whoever, that is dependent upon them, because we've been so dependent upon them serving us and securing our freedom.

There's a lot of great companies out there that donate or have a cause like Toms shoes. You buy a pair; they give a pair away.

I'm a big proponent that if you start looking at what's going on with the past and present military, whether they're homeless or struggling with routine life, trying to find a way to make things happen, that's how we change what's going on here in the United States.

Go to https://notebuyingblueprint.com/book to get into the Note Buying Blueprint – Note Genius Suite and give a free ticket to a military member at the same time. If you know someone in the military that would like this opportunity, you can sponsor them, or if not, we will give a free membership to a military personnel that has expressed interest in buying notes and is waiting to get started!

ABOUT THE AUTHOR

Scott Carson has been an active real estate investor since 2002 and a full time investor since 2005.

He has been in the finance industry since 2001 as a mortgage banker and financial advisor for over a decade. He is the President of WeCloseNotes.com Inc., an Austin-based, note buying company specializing in buying defaulted mortgages on residential and commercial properties from over 5000 banks and hedge funds across the country.

He is also the creator of the Note Buying for Dummies workshop that focuses on teaching investors the Three F's of Note Buying.... How Find, Fund, and Flip NPN's.

He is a regular contributor to Investor's Business Daily and has been quoted in the Wall Street Journal along with being a featured speaker at the National Association of Realtors conference, National Association of Real Estate Investor Clubs, and the Annual Noteworthy Convention where he was awarded the Note Educator of the Year.

Besides being a national and international speaker on buying notes, he is also a specialist on short sales and raising private capital for investors across the country.

When he isn't reading, writing or buying notes and real estate for his or his students' portfolios, you can find him traveling, writing, playing golf, attending sporting events or spending time with his friends.